Nonprofit Quick Guide™

How to Advance in Your Fundraising Career

Linda Lysakowski, ACFRE
Joanne Oppelt, MHA

Nonprofit Quick Guide: How to Advance in Your Fundraising Career

One of the **Nonprofit Quick Guide**™ series

Published by Joanne Oppelt Consulting, LLC

ISBN Print Book: 978-1-951978-00-6

13 12 11 10 9 8 7 6 5 4 3 2 1

Printed in the United States of America

About the Authors

LINDA LYSAKOWSKI, ACFRE

Linda is one of approximately one hundred professionals worldwide to hold the Advanced Certified Fundraising Executive designation. Linda is the author of ten nonfiction books, a contributing author, coeditor, or coauthor of fifteen others. She has also written three books in the fiction realm.

Linda has more than thirty years in the development field. She worked for a university and a museum before starting her own consulting firm. In her twenty-five years as a philanthropic consultant, Linda has managed capital campaigns that have raised more than $50 million, helped hundreds of nonprofit organizations achieve their development goals, and trained more than forty thousand development professionals in most of the fifty states of the United States, Canada, Mexico, Egypt, and Bermuda.

She served on the Association of Fundraising Philanthropy (AFP) Foundation for Philanthropy Board and on the Professional Advancement Division for AFP. She is a past president of the Eastern Pennsylvania and Sierra (Nevada) AFP chapters. She received the Outstanding Fundraiser of the Year award from the Eastern Pennsylvania, Las Vegas, and Sierra (Nevada) chapters of AFP, was honored with the Barbara Marion Award for Outstanding Service to AFP, and received the Lifetime Achievement Award from the Las Vegas AFP chapter.

Linda is a graduate of Alvernia University with majors in banking and finance as well as theology/philosophy, and a minor in communications. As a graduate of AFP's Faculty Training Academy, she is a Master Teacher.

JOANNE OPPELT, MHA

Joanne, principal of Joanne Oppelt Consulting, LLC, is a seasoned rainmaker with a distinguished track record of success. During her twenty-five-plus years working in the nonprofit arena, she built or rebuilt successful fundraising departments at every stop, helping her organizations grow capacity and more effectively fulfill their missions.

She has held positions from grantwriter to executive director at the nonprofits Community Access Unlimited, Caring Contact: A Listening Community, Family to Family Network of New Jersey, Christian Healthcare Center, March of Dimes Central New Jersey, Prevent Child Abuse New Jersey, and Maternal and Family Health Services. Her extensive background in a variety of work roles and organizations enables her to understand the realities and challenges nonprofit practitioners face–both internally and externally. Her success at every stop positions her to help any nonprofit, whether through her books or consulting practice, turn around its struggling fundraising operations.

Joanne is the author of four books and coauthor of one. She has taught at Kean University as an Adjunct Professor in its graduate program. She is also a highly sought-after speaker and presenter.

Joanne holds a master's degree in health administration from Wilkes University, where she graduated with distinction. Her bachelor's degree is in education, with a minor in psychology.

Dedication

Dedicated to the thousands of nonprofit fundraisers engaged in the noble work of changing lives and saving lives.

Contents

Chapter One

What Does It Mean to Work in the Nonprofit Sector?

L et Linda tell you about how she entered the profession of fundraising; it may be a familiar story to some of you. Back in the 1970s, she was a banker. Most banks, partly because of the Community Reinvestment Act and partly because they wanted to be good corporate citizens, encouraged their employees to be active volunteers in their communities.

Like many other bank employees, Linda eagerly volunteered for numerous fundraising activities, including working on her alma mater's annual business appeal. This was the first time she realized that there was a profession of fundraising; that people actually got paid to ask for money!

"Gee," Linda thought, "I've been doing it as a volunteer for many years and loved the feeling of satisfaction that came with obtaining a commitment for a gift to the annual appeal, working on a successful fundraising event, talking to a group of business colleagues about the great work a nonprofit was doing in our community. Wow, I could get paid to do this???!!! How hard could this be if volunteers could do it?"

Then one day, she opened her file drawer at work to look for a file for a project she was working on for the bank and realized there were more files in her drawer for her volunteer nonprofit activities than there were for work projects. Perhaps it was time for a career change! Before she knew it, she found herself as Assistant Vice President for Institutional Advancement at her alma mater.

Linda quickly found out there was more to fundraising than she had imagined. Not long after starting her new career, she attended a CASE (Council for the Advancement and Support of Education) conference and had to quickly learn terms with which she was not familiar—LYBUNTS,

SYBUNTS, fulfillment rates, nonprofit bulk rate indicia, planned giving, and many more.

"What have I gotten myself into?" she asked.

Linda found that, while her business background was beneficial, the nonprofit sector was a very different world.

Joanne's story is very different than Linda's. Joanne didn't know what she wanted to do. At first, she thought she would be a medical doctor. But she didn't quite comprehend all the advanced sciences necessary to enter medical school. So, instead, she got her degree in education and decided to be a teacher. Joanne felt that teaching would give her the flexibility she needed to balance a career and family. Until she was actually hired to teach in a classroom and didn't like it. While she liked making a difference in the lives of children, following a curriculum wasn't her thing. So, she went back to school and studied health administration.

Graduate school gave her the experience to explore both the insurance and government sides of addressing community health issues. Neither was a good fit for her. While she was driven to do good, she didn't want to make profit-driven decisions about people's lives. Nor did she want to work in a vast political bureaucracy. So, after graduation, Joanne started her professional career in nonprofits. Her first professional job was at a regional maternal and child health agency in northeast Pennsylvania.

When she interviewed for the job, Joanne was given a choice between working as an education manager or an as-yet-undefined role of a program manager. She chose the program manager position. The only direction she was given was that thing the agency wanted to expand. She pretty much had to figure things out for herself. So, she started contacting other community agencies with an interest in maternal and child health to see if they would all like to address issues together. That caught the attention of the local government officials. Within a month, Joanne was also given a failed state grant to rewrite and resubmit. She did and, to her surprise, it was funded. She has worked in nonprofit fundraising ever since.

The Nonprofit Sector

For clarification purposes, let's start with what it means to work for a nonprofit organization. In the United States, a charitable nonprofit is usually a 501(c)(3) agency, a designation received from the Internal Revenue Service after meeting certain requirements, most importantly that the organization serves a charitable, education, scientific, or community service purpose. Individuals may be able to deduct donations to approved nonprofit organizations when filing their federal tax returns.

Most government agencies and foundations will only make grants to nonprofit organizations.

Contrary to popular opinion, being a nonprofit does not mean that the organization must operate in the red or that it cannot have a fund surplus. As a nonprofit, you can realize a budget surplus. Nonprofit is a tax determination, not a business plan.

So, before you think working in fundraising means you get paid peanuts and must beg for money, know that is not true. Get rid of that thinking if you want to succeed at fundraising.

Sometimes the nonprofit community is called the third sector (as opposed to government or the business sector), the independent sector, or the voluntary sector. All these terms are appropriate and accurate. Some nonprofits are thought of as charities, while some are massive operations such as major universities and health care systems. They share the commonality of being a nonprofit entity since no individual or group of individuals benefit from the surplus revenues of the organization.

Nonprofits employ about 10 percent of the workforce in the United States. It is big business!

So, Why Fundraising?

Fundraising has been around for more years than many people realize. Some of the founders of the United States are those who can be considered some of this country's first professional fundraisers, including Benjamin Franklin. These founders worked tirelessly to raise money to build hospitals and schools in this new country that rivaled those of their European homelands. For many years, it was mostly the larger institutions of higher learning and health care that employed paid fundraisers.

In recent years, however, this has all changed. Today, many nonprofit organizations employ at least one development professional, and fundraising is becoming a respected career. The larger institutions often employ dozens of fundraisers. Still, some people may feel that fundraising as a career is just one step above that of a used-car salesperson. Or perhaps even one step below!

There is an old saying in fundraising: "No money, no mission."

This means that fundraising is just as important as the programs the nonprofit operates because without fundraising, most organizations would not be able to run their programs, even those such as universities, hospitals, and others that collect fees for service. And some are dependent on fundraising as their only source of income.

Philanthropy, literally the "love of humankind," has been described as voluntary action for the common good. It also includes those of us who work in the profession, along with volunteers and donors.

So, never be ashamed of your career in fundraising. It is vital work that we do.

Wrapping It Up

- The nonprofit world is big business, employing 10 percent of the workforce in the United States.
- Fundraising has been around since the beginning of this country.
- Fundraising is necessary for most nonprofits.
- Be proud of your career as a fundraiser, you are doing noble work!

Chapter Two

What Does It Take to Succeed in Fundraising?

What are the key characteristics of a successful fundraiser? Are these characteristics inborn, or can they be acquired? What can you, as a fundraising professional, do to acquire or strengthen these characteristics within yourself? What do you look for when hiring development staff people?

Many individuals entering the profession for the first time, as well as those hiring their first development staff person, are often not certain what qualities to look for in a suitable candidate. Often one hears that development is really just sales or marketing. The individual or organization about to embark into the world of development needs to understand that it is a profession in its own right. Being a good salesperson or a good marketer may be helpful in fundraising, but there is far more to the career than sales and marketing. In his book, *Born to Raise,* the late Jerold Panas lists the top ten qualities of a successful fundraiser as:

- Impeccable integrity
- Good listener
- Ability to motivate
- Hard worker
- Concern for people
- High expectations
- Love the work
- High energy
- Perseverance
- Presence

This is a tall order—what if you feel you do not have these qualities? Can they be learned? If so, how can you learn to cultivate them? Let's look at each one and see if there are things that can be done to cultivate what might seem, at first glance, like innate qualities. We first want to address the one area we both think is critical and that is integrity.

Impeccable Integrity

Although professional integrity seems to be a quality that one either has or doesn't, there are things you can do to help develop your personal integrity. First know, understand, and support the AFP (Association of Fundraising Professionals) Code of Ethics and Standards of Professional Practice. These documents will provide guidelines about what is ethical in the field of fundraising. Adherence to the Donor Bill of Rights is another step in assuring that the organization holds the donor's interests above its own and that you, the professional, hold the interests of the donor first, the organization second, and yourself last.

If you have a faith system, it can help in developing your sense of morality and ethics. Every major religious belief system holds certain moral principles that can help its members make sound ethical judgments.

You can also enroll in an ethics class or attend AFP ethics programs. AFP also has an ethics board that can answer questions about ethical issues. So, although integrity might seem to be an inborn quality, it can be developed by understanding ethics, morals, and donors' rights. One thing that can help you develop professional integrity is to follow the hierarchy of judging whether a specific action, including the acceptance of a major gift, values the donor's interest above your interest, and even above the interest of the organization for which you work.

Hierarchy of Integrity

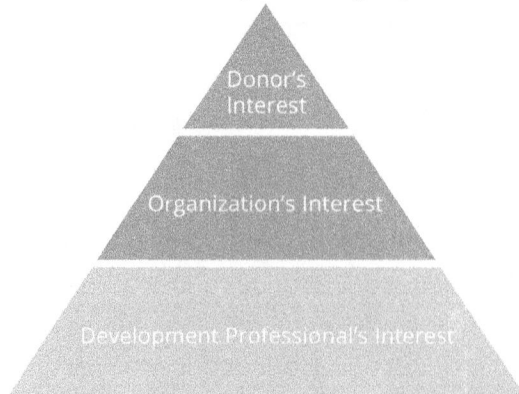

Good Listener

Good listening is definitely a quality that can be learned. A class in communications can help emphasize that listening is the most critical part of excellent communication skills. (There may be a very good reason why human beings were created with one mouth and two ears!)

Active listening is vital to good donor relations. Often, a major gift can be secured by a solicitor whose listening skills have been honed. Listening for what the donor's interests are is even more important than being able to persuasively explain the organization's case. Practice making "the ask" and truly listening to the donor through role playing with colleagues or by attending courses in making the ask.

Ability to Motivate

The ability to motivate donors, volunteers, and staff is a critical key for success. Motivating donors goes back to the integrity section. Putting the donor's interest first and foremost will make it easier for you to motivate donors. Motivating donors does not mean persuading donors to do something that they don't want to do or is not in their best interest. Motivating donors comes through understanding that philanthropy brings joy to the donor and that if the donor really believes in the mission, motivation is simply a tool to bring about the donor's wishes. Learning the case for support and having passion for the mission of the organization for which one works are the best ways to successfully motivate another person to share that passion.

It is also important for you to understand the psychology of philanthropy. There are many motivating factors that prompt an individual to contribute to a nonprofit organization. Each donor will have different motivating factors that influence a decision to give or not give. Listening to the donor is a critical skill which can help you understand how to motivate donors. Volunteers, likewise, can be motivated only if the volunteers and the fundraising staff share a passion for the mission of the organization. Again, a good course in communication will help you learn how to speak and write with enthusiasm and passion that will motivate others.

Motivating the staff of the organization is also important. This starts with having respect and concern for other staff members. Staff members will be motivated by the good example set by the chief development officer. Involving staff in the development planning process is a good way to motivate them to help implement the plan.

Regular staff meetings that include an educational segment about some facet of fundraising, including an occasional motivational or inspirational guest speaker, in addition to staff updates on current projects, can help motivate staff to greatness.

Hard Worker

One thing you need to understand going into this profession is that it is definitely not a nine-to-five job. Often you may be on the job as early as 7 a.m. meeting with volunteers, attending breakfast meetings, or just getting into the office early to organize your day before the phone calls and emails start arriving. You may easily be at work until 7 or 9 p.m. attending after-hours events, meeting with volunteers, or working at a phonathon. The key is to work hard but take good care of yourself at the same time. Eating healthy, getting regular exercise, having a hobby or interests outside of work, and taking a vacation (or several mini vacations) each year will keep you mentally and physically healthy even though the hours of your job may be demanding.

And, working hard does not mean you need to be "wired in" 24/7. Leave work at work. Do not take it home or on vacation unless it is extremely critical. In some cases, it might be better to answer emails while on vacation rather than becoming stressed out by the sheer volume of email waiting at the office on your first day back at work. But, as a true professional, be careful to avoid thinking that you are indispensable and that you always must stay connected to the office.

You aren't, and you don't!

Concern for People

Again, this may seem like an innate quality that one either has or doesn't, but there are some things you can do to cultivate concern for people.

First, working for an organization about which you care deeply is one way that you can feel concern for the organization's clients. Many professionals gravitate to an organization that may have helped them or a loved one and these individuals will usually be empathetic with the organization's clients.

Another tool that can help is to get out and about within the organization, the old "management by walking around" theory. Talk to the people who use your organization's services, find out their stories, and talk to them about their hopes and desires for the future. It will make fundraising easier and allow you to speak in a compelling fashion about your organization's mission and can also help you build empathy and concern.

Concern for people goes beyond caring about the donors and the clients but extends as well into concern for the staff. Taking time to listen to the concerns of other staff people, your colleagues in the development office and others in the organization, can help the development professional build a concern for people.

High Expectations

As a development professional, you should have high expectations not only for yourself, but for your organization and for your coworkers. Often it is the development professional that "leads from the middle" and inspires the organization to greatness. Cultivating donors who have vision is one way to lead the organization to a higher level of performance. Also, some board members can have a great effect on the vision of the organization, so as a development professional you should have input into the selection of new board members who can help transform the organization into bigger and better things. However, this does not mean setting unrealistic goals or having expectations that are so demanding that the board, volunteers, and staff get frustrated.

Expecting the best from the development staff, and other staff within the organization, is critical as well. Development professionals who have a staff reporting to them should allow the staff members to set their own goals and provide them with the tools to do their job. Having a once-a-year staff retreat for the development office members in addition to regular staff meetings can be a good way to empower staff.

Love the Work

Not only do you need to love the organization you work for, you need to love the work of development! Loving this career often starts with volunteering in the area of development. If you do not enjoy volunteer fundraising, you probably won't love it as a career. So, if you are just thinking about entering the profession, you may want to begin by volunteering to work on a special event, a phonathon, or a business appeal for a few nonprofits and see if you really do love fundraising.

As with anything, the more knowledgeable you become in an area, the more likely it is you will enjoy doing it. Who can say they love knitting if they don't know how to knit, or cooking if they have never learned how to cook, or skiing if they haven't taken a ski lesson? The same is true with development. You will need to learn as much as you can about the profession by taking classes, reading books, attending workshops. If you find a particular aspect of fundraising that really appeals to you, such as planned giving, major gifts, or grant writing, you should pursue that area. If you prefer being a generalist, you should look for a position as a development director in a small shop where you will get to do a variety of fundraising tasks. Finding your niche is critical to loving the work. It also means that if you become frustrated, worn out, or just bored, you may need to think about moving on.

High Energy

Having high energy seems like a natural for some people, whereas for others, it may require some work. But energy can be built by following some of the advice mentioned earlier. Eating right, exercising, and relieving stress by taking time off can help boost your energy.

Using artificial stimulants like caffeine does not really give you a high energy level and may, in fact, cause the opposite when the temporary effects of caffeine wear off. A good herbal tea that relaxes may actually do more to boost your energy. Getting enough sleep at night also helps raise your energy levels during the day. Simple things like having nice artwork or an essential oil diffuser in your office, or taking time off work to get a pedicure, can help build energy.

Loving the work will also help you have the high energy needed to work long hours; motivate donors, volunteers, and staff; and meet the expectations you have set for yourself or others have set for you.

Perseverance

One thing that senior development professionals have learned is that perseverance is a highly needed quality. Major and planned gifts, in particular, require building long-term relationships; perseverance pays off. If donors think the organization has forgotten about them, they may just move on to the next organization.

If your development office needs to undergo a computer conversion, perseverance is definitely going to be required! This is a tedious and frustrating process and one that never seems to be completed in the expected timeframe.

So how do you cultivate perseverance? Part of the secret to perseverance is setting goals and realistic benchmarks to measure success. This will keep you from wanting to throw in the towel when the going gets tough. Strategic planning is one way to develop reasonable timelines for yourself, and help you understand that often good things take time. CEOs and development officers are often under a great deal of pressure to raise money quickly. Entrepreneurial board members who are shrewd businesspeople are often accustomed to working based on instant decisions and may want the development officer to just "go out and do it" without adequate planning.

Be careful not to get so caught up in keeping your head above water that you do not have the time to plan. A recent survey asking development professionals what their biggest challenge is shows that lack of time for planning is the leading challenge listed.

Working on long-term goals for a specific amount of time each day can help. And understanding that you should focus 90-95 percent of your time on the 5-10 percent of donors who account for 90-95 percent of all the gifts your organization will receive helps as well.

Of course, sometimes the organization itself needs to cultivate patience and persistence, so helping to build a philanthropic culture within the organization is a big part of your role. One of your major tasks may be helping your board and executive staff understand that fundraising is all about building relationships and that if you persevere in this relationship building, your organization will benefit tremendously. If you can impart this knowledge to your organization's leaders, you will rise to the top of your field. You must take the time to plan strategically; otherwise your organization will be left behind in the dynamic and ever-evolving world of the nonprofit sector. Leadership should look at the return on investment of careful, strategic planning.

Presence

This may be the hardest to define and the hardest to cultivate in a development professional. Perhaps the closest thing to this may be a "perception of poise." A more contemporary definition may be closer to "positioning yourself." Presence can also be described as the ability to command attention and being respected as a professional.

So. what can you do to develop a sense of presence?

First, always look and act professional. Development professionals, especially when meeting with donors or potential donors (which may be all the time), should wear a suit and tie, or for women, a suit, nice dress, or pant suit. Although some nonprofits adopt a more casual atmosphere, dressing for success is important for the development professional because you will be very visible in the community. And of course, you never know when that million-dollar donor may walk in the front door! Being well dressed and well-groomed will give you the sense of pride and confidence that is necessary for a sense of presence. This does not necessarily mean you need to spend a lot of money on clothes and new car but looking good and driving a respectable looking car can help add a sense of presence. Good posture and an open and welcoming facial expression can be very meaningful, especially when you remember that you only have one opportunity to make a first impression!

Of course, presence is about much more than just looking good. Knowing the job will make you appear more confident and knowledgeable, adding to the presence factor. So, not to belabor the point, education and training are critical. Read, attend workshops, and join a professional organization such as AFP!

Wrapping It Up

Some practical tips to help you become successful at fundraising:

- Make a conscious decision to work only for organizations whose mission you feel passionate about. Remember the adage: do what you love, and the money will follow.

- Strive to be a change agent within the organization for which you work. Develop a plan to educate the organization's leadership about philanthropy.

- Remember that the donor's interest is always the foremost consideration in any decisions involving fundraising.

- As we've discussed, there are several key traits that successful fundraisers have in common. These traits include impeccable integrity; being a good listener; the ability to motivate staff, volunteers and donors; being a hard worker; having a true concern for people; having high expectations for yourself, your organization and other people including staff, volunteers and donors; perseverance; and presence. While some of these might seem to be innate qualities, there are things you can do to develop them.

- Success is measured in many ways—financial success, personal growth, happiness, and a feeling of doing a job well, and making a difference. How do *you* measure success?

Chapter Three

Specialist or Generalist?

One of the things that can help you succeed in fundraising is asking yourself the question, "What is which is more attractive to me—being a generalist or a specialist?"

One of the advantages of working in a small organization is that for those who enjoy being a generalist, the one-person development office offers an opportunity to learn about all the aspects of development, from Internet fundraising to planned giving and capital campaigns. Many people thrive on that type of atmosphere; they really enjoy doing a little bit of everything. We know that we both prefer this type of work! Doing something different every day and learning about all kinds of fundraising.

And it is a great way to learn about the various types of careers in fundraising that might develop into a desire to specialize in one of these aspects. Also, running a one-person shop often is a good training ground for moving into a position of supervising a staff of development people or even preparing for a career as an executive director or a consultant.

So, what are some typical specialties one finds in the development office?

Major Gifts

Major gifts are generally defined as a gift at level that requires special treatment, such as personal solicitation, special recognition, etc. Major gift levels are defined differently by each organization. In a university or large nonprofit, a major gift could be $100,000 or even $1 million, and in some smaller organizations, a major gift might be $500 or even $100.

Most organizations value individuals who have had experience in obtaining major gifts and have a track record of success. (Note that major gifts are defined very differently for each organization.) But if you enjoy meeting face-to-face with individual donors, you may opt to specialize in major gifts.

Financial planners, attorneys, and bankers often find this career path attractive, particularly if they have dealt with high-income clients in a former career. For example, Linda's career in private banking was much akin to working with major donors. This is a highly sought-after specialty that generally comes only after years in the field. However, many development professionals in entry level positions strive to learn as much as possible about major gifts fundraising so they can specialize in this area.

Planned Giving

Planned gifts may be thought of as major gifts that are often not given outright (like a major gift is) but, rather, are structured in some way. For example, a donor may place real estate into a charitable trust for the ultimate benefit of the organization at the donor's death. Or a donor may make the most common planned gift of all, a gift to the organization designated in the donor's will or living trust.

Because gift planning is a discipline requiring training and experience, it is a career path often chosen by attorneys, financial planners, or bankers who want to leave the for-profit world and work in development.

While not usually as high paying as a career in law or the financial world, it is generally one of the highest paid positions in the profession of fundraising.

Many of these professionals find that, although there is a significant cut in salary compared to the typical earning level of attorneys and financial planners, they enjoy the nonprofit world because of a passion for the mission or just because they want to leave the corporate world behind them.

Many attorneys and bankers who have left the corporate world report that they are much happier in the nonprofit community where they feel they are really making a difference.

Campaign Specialist/Director/Manager

Some people really enjoy the fast-paced world of capital campaigns and, in a large organization like a university where campaigns are usually perpetual, there may be openings for people who work exclusively on capital campaigns and special projects. Once you develop experience in capital campaigns for one organization, you can easily move into becoming a capital campaign specialist in a larger organization where capital campaigns are prevalent, or even into a consulting career.

Annual Giving

Many individuals enjoy the annual giving part of fundraising. While some may think that it is boring and repetitious, the annual giving program is the key to developing major donors. In a smaller organization, positions in this area might involve managing the direct mail program, a telephone program, and Internet fundraising or, in a larger organization, managing just one of these components. An "annual fund generalist" who works in all aspects of the annual fund may find that one area is particularly appealing and may decide to focus even more narrowly on direct mail, for example. Positions with a narrow focus like this tend to be available in very large organizations.

Corporate/Business Giving

Many individuals, particularly those who came into the fundraising profession from the business world, will find corporate/business giving challenging and rewarding.

This area of fundraising may include drafting proposals for corporate foundations or organizing an annual business appeal.

If you come from a business background, your contacts can prove valuable to the nonprofit organization seeking corporate support. As a businessperson entering the fundraising profession, your experience in the business world may be attractive to an organization that is trying to increase the level of its corporate/business fundraising efforts.

This was one area of fundraising that both Linda and Joanne particularly enjoy due to their respective professional and educational backgrounds in business.

Special Events

Some people just love throwing parties, and although there is a lot more involved in running special events than being present at the event itself, including seeking sponsorships, managing the calendar, preparing the budget, recruiting and working with volunteers, special events may appeal to you. If you have volunteered at the organization's special events, you may be interested in working as a staff person coordinating events.

Because special events can be so labor-intensive and draining, staff members who start in this position may often seek to move into more integrated fundraising roles where they have an opportunity to work on various fundraising projects in addition to events. But, for others, this is a specialty they want to make their career. And they may even consider consulting on special events.

Writing

If your passion is the written word, there are positions in development for grant proposal writers and those who can write a good case for support, as well as other fundraising materials developed from the case. Journalism majors or people who have worked in the media often look for a career writing for nonprofits. Many larger organizations offer this specialty. In smaller organizations, the development officers may do all the writing themselves or may outsource some of this to an outside contractor. Another option for those who someday want to consult.

Research

If you enjoy doing research and working with data, there are opportunities to research individuals, businesses, and foundations. Those with technical skills, good logic, and persistence may find this an ideal development position. Universities and other large organizations generally have a department of researchers. Again, in smaller organizations, this task usually falls under the chief development officer's duties or might be outsourced. However, this is another option for consultants.

Data Entry/Donor Management

If you are skilled at managing data, you may find this position rewarding. Managing a donor database is one of the key positions in any development office, so a good database manager may be a highly sought-after individual. This position includes preparing development office reports, and sometimes research as well as stewardship of donor records. Individuals interested in technology and the Internet, and who have great organization skills, may be well suited for this position. Today's CRM (customer relationship management) programs are so user-friendly, however, that many development officers manage the database. Usually, only the larger institutions will have someone solely devoted to data management.

Position titles will vary from organization to organization, and there may be variations of any or all the above positions. But in a larger development office, there is generally a chief development officer, vice president, or director of development who manages the rest of the staff. In a small office, the director of development will likely be responsible for all these tasks.

Wrapping It Up

Some practical tips to help you find your niche:
- Take a personality test and find out if you are a person who sees the big picture or if you really like to get into the details.

- Talk to people in the development profession and ask them what they like and don't like about their jobs and what their biggest challenges and greatest rewards are.
- Volunteer at a large organization to help in its development office and get a flavor for all that it takes to run a large development program.
- There is no right answer to whether you should be a specialist or a generalist. Do what works for you.

Chapter Four

Educating Yourself

When we first entered the wonderful world of philanthropy back in the dark ages (before email, can you believe that?), we realized if we wanted to advance in this career (and we did want that), we simply had to follow the same three steps Linda followed when she advanced rapidly in her banking career.

They are simple steps, but not necessarily *easy*—they require some work on your part. They are:

1. Learn
2. Get Involved
3. Set Goals for Yourself

Sound simple? Well, it is much easier today than it was back in 1988 when Linda started in fundraising.

Learn

First, learn as much as you can.

When Linda started her first development job as assistant vice president of institutional advancement (what a mouthful), she realized she had a lot of business and sales experience but knew little about development, fundraising, and philanthropy—other than what she knew from her volunteer involvement.

When Joanne started in nonprofits, she also knew little about fundraising. Her background had prepared her for healthcare administration, not development.

How about you? Whether you came into *your* job through another nonprofit career, a career in the for-profit world, or volunteer work, there are probably areas of this field that you know a lot about and others that you need to learn.

As we mentioned, Linda was fortunate enough to have a boss who, early on, sent her to a CASE (Council for the Advancement and Support of Education) conference and when they started throwing around terms like LYBUNT and SYBUNT, she said, "huh?" Joanne's first training experience involved grantsmanship. She had to learn what SMART objectives and logic models are. Most likely, there are terms you might not be familiar with, too. Our best advice is to emulate SpongeBob SquarePants. Take advantage of learning opportunities and soak it all up like a sponge.

When Linda attended her first conference, she had to drive from Pennsylvania to New Hampshire, stay in a dorm room, and sit in classes for several days. But she loved the fact that she was exposed to a new set of people and learned tons of new information. The next year, she attended her first AFP International conference in San Antonio and was hooked from that moment on. She participated in every conference since then that she could. However, today you can sit in your office or at home and take webinars, attend symposia, and even take courses.

Formal Education

When we entered this field, there were no colleges or university programs designed to train people in fundraising. You learned on the job. Today there are undergraduate and graduate programs in nonprofit management and in development/philanthropy. You can even earn a PhD in philanthropy.

Almost all local colleges and universities have a nonprofit management program, either a certificate program or an undergraduate degree. Check your local colleges and see what they have available. A search on the Internet will give you resources for graduate and undergraduate programs in nonprofit management, which are suitable for executive directors and other staff, as well as those that specialize in fundraising/development philanthropy. For these more specialized degree programs, you may have to go out of state or online.

In selecting a learning program, we recommend that you consider whether the instructors are professionals in the field or academics who have knowledge of philanthropy but have not actually worked in the field. While academics can teach you a lot, you may want someone who has worked in the fundraising field, as well.

Workshops, Conferences, Seminars, Symposia

There is a lot of excellent training you can get on a less formal basis than getting a degree. AFP's annual International Conference (ICON) draws thousands of fundraisers from all over the world. Those who are in specialized fields such as church fundraising, hospital fundraising, higher education, etc. can attend conferences where the audience is comprised of people who work in that fled. The American Association of Museums, CASE, Association of Healthcare Philanthropy (AHP), Association of Lutheran Development Officer (ALDE), and National Catholic Development Conference (NCDC) are just a few examples of where you can get more specialized training focused on your organization's needs. And many specialized national organizations such as Court Appointed Special Advocates (CASA) and Down Syndrome Affiliates in Action (DSAIA), Big Brothers Big Sister (BBBS) typically have national conferences at which fundraising is one topic that is addressed among other areas that relate to these organizations.

There are also statewide organizations such as associations of nonprofits, for example, the Maryland Association of Nonprofit Organizations (MANO). Almost every state has a similar organization and those annual conferences typically cover fundraising as well as other topics relevant to nonprofits. There are also many statewide coalitions such as Nevada Coalition to End Domestic and Sexual Violence (NCEDSV), who focus on a narrow field, may be more affordable than traveling to a national or international conference.

Local AFP chapters also typically hold monthly meetings, and most offer an annual one- or two-day conference.

Take advantage of these opportunities. Not only are they a great place to earn but are also valuable networking opportunities.

Online Learning

Online learning is probably our favorite! After years of speaking at conferences and workshops, we still love being there in person and getting to meet everyone and share their stories. But in practicality, conferences can be expensive when you count the travel time and expenses, in addition to the conference fees. So, we began teaching webinars. Linda then branched out into offering full-blown online courses on a variety of fundraising topics.

Today you can avail yourself of a ton on free webinars, including both of ours, of course. But if you want more intense training, you will have to pay fees, though the fees may not be as much as you think. For example, Linda currently offers fourteen courses for a low monthly subscription fee. We invite you to learn more at https://www.lindalysakowski.com. The advantage of online courses, in addition to saving a ton of money, is that you can take them at your own pace from home, work, Starbucks, or any convenient location.

Wrapping It Up

- Learn, Learn, Learn. Trust us, you don't know it all!
- If you want a degree in fundraising/development/philanthropy, check your local colleges and universities and if you can't find one that offers degree programs, search the Internet.
- Attend conferences and workshops. Not only is there valuable information to be gained, but networking opportunities abound.
- Online learning is more affordable and far more convenient.

Chapter Five

Getting Certified

One of the best ways to enhance your personal growth in the development profession is to look at the certification process. Fundraisers who have been in the field for five years or longer may be eligible to become a CFRE (Certified Fund Raising Executive). This certification has become a respected designation in the field, and many job opportunities may require certification or, at the very least, the job posting will state, "CFRE preferred." Talk to some CFREs you know. According to CFRE International, 94 percent of CFREs say the sense of personal achievement provided by CFRE certification has been valuable to their career and 81 percent of CFREs say earning their CFRE enhanced their credibility with employers and clients.

What are the Requirements to Become a CFRE?

Education – you will need to provide documentation of a minimum of eighty points, consisting of formal education, professional development/continuing education attended, or volunteer service during the most recent five years.

Professional Practice – you will also be required to provide documentation of a minimum of thirty-six points, the equivalent of three years of full-time or half-time experience as a paid, professional fundraiser during the most recent five years. This employment is to be a paid, professional member of a fundraising staff or a fundraising consultant for a nonprofit organization with at least 50 percent full-time, or 100 percent half-time, of job duties and responsibilities assigned to fundraising activities, resource development and/or the management of fund development which results in the generation of philanthropic support. CFRE defines half-time employment as one-half full-time employment (FTE) or greater. Professional experience in this category must have taken place during the most recent five years, which allows for gaps in employment. Political fundraising is not considered eligible for points in this category.

Written Test—you will be required to take a written exam, which is typically done online.

Ethics—the CFRE board will review your application and your exam and certify that there are no ethics violations that have been filed against you.

For more information on the certification process, check out CFRE International at www.cfre.org.

The ACFRE Process

If you have been in the field for more than ten years and are already a CFRE, the Advanced Certified Fund Raising Executive (ACFRE) is a highly respected designation currently held by slightly more than one hundred professionals worldwide. Although the process is rigorous, it is rewarding both personally and financially for many individuals.

Candidates for the ACFRE must present:

- a copy of their current resume or Curriculum Vitae
- A copy of the letter confirming they are currently a CFRE, FAHP, IADF (International Advanced Diploma in Fundraising), or evidence of a minimum of twenty years full-time professional experience in fundraising.

ACFRE candidates who do not hold a bachelor's degree will be required to have evidence of fifteen years in the field, instead of ten.

During the ACFRE process, in addition to proof of experience, you will complete a written exam, and if a passing grade is obtained, you will need to submit a portfolio of your work and pass an oral exam conducted by ACFRE. And, of course, any breach of ethical standards will disqualify you from obtaining your ACFRE.

To find out more about this process, contact AFP at www.afpnet.org.

The possession of a certification credential correlated positively with salary. Fundraisers in the United States possessing the Certified Fund Raising Executive (CFRE) credential earned, on average, $19,000 more than respondents with no certification, while individuals in Canada holding the credential earned C$14,000 more than those who did not. Those individuals possessing the Advanced Certified Fund Raising Executive (ACFRE) credential earned $48,000 more in the U.S. and $24,000 more in Canada.

Most CFREs and ACFREs say they received certification mainly for personal satisfaction, but the increased salary and credibility that come along with certification are certainly a plus.

Wrapping it Up

- If you are in the fundraising field more than five years, you should investigate the CFRE process
- If you have ten years or more in the field, consider the ACFRE designation
- Certification gives you more credibility with your employer, prospective employer, or clients if you are a consultant.
- CFREs and ACFREs earn more money than their counterparts.

Chapter Six

Getting Involved

I n addition to providing us with training, the other wise thing our first bosses did was to have us to get involved in the profession. Joanne joined her local AFP chapter and is still a member. Linda joined three chapters of AFP and got very active in two of them; before long, she was president of her local chapter. Not long after that, she became active on the national and international level of AFP and served on the board of the AFP Foundation for Philanthropy. Not only did this help her advance her career, but she made many life-long friends who still support her in her work and personal life.

Then, just as she was starting her consulting business in 1993, CharityChannel was also getting started, and she got involved in it as soon as she heard about it. Joanne found CharityChannel in 2008. Another whole avenue of networking possibility opened and again, they found life-long friendships, such as the one that prompted us to team up on this series of books, as well as opportunities to grow and advance in their careers.

In What Organizations Should I Get Involved?

First, look at your professional organization, whether it is AFP, CASE, AHP, or whatever association you or your organization belong to that focuses on fundraising. Serve on a committee, speak at a conference, attend meetings and network with your peers, and get involved at a regional or national level. The experience will help you grow in your profession. The networking opportunities may present you with new career options. And, you will be giving back to your profession.

Look at organizations that focus on your organization's particular field, such as the American Library Association, the Association of American Museums, and the like. If you are committed to the field, this is a great way you learn more and become more valuable to your current employer. And, again, it may open the door to other positions within larger organizations. And, if you become a consultant, you may want to focus on a specific type of nonprofit.

You should also look at organizations outside your field, which will help you make contacts. One thing we always recommend is getting involved in your local Chamber of Commerce. This is the best way to contact business leaders that can support your organization. Your community may also have an economic development council or manufacturers association. All of these are great ways to make contact with your local business communities.

Again, it is not just joining these organizations. It is getting involved. Volunteer to serve on a committee. Attend meetings. Don't forget to carry plenty of business cards. Introduce yourself to other members. We always make it a habit to sit at different tables and meet new members at each meeting or get-together.

You might also get involved in speaking to service and professional groups such as Rotary, Lions' Clubs, Sertoma, Kiwanis, or Soroptimists, among others. Getting involved opens up a great opportunity to make new friends for your organization and also for yourself. You never know when these networking opportunities will come in handy.

Wrapping It Up

- Join a professional fundraising organization, and volunteer to serve on committees, hold office, or speak at meetings.
- If your organization belongs to an organization for your specific field, get involved and volunteer for that organization.
- Look at service clubs and professional organizations in your community, but don't just join, get involved.

Chapter Seven

Setting Goals

Okay, we saved the best for last: setting goals for yourself.
Development officers should be very familiar with goal setting—annual fund goals, capital campaign goals, major gift goals, donor retention goals, constituent participation goals. But how often have you focused on setting goals for *yourself*?

Being Type A personalities, we have always set goals for ourselves. When Linda entered this field, her goals were ambitious, but she fulfilled them all. Her goals were:

- Become a CFRE
- Become an ACFRE
- Become a national speaker
- Travel
- Become a consultant
- Write a book
- Leave a legacy

Joanne's goals were different. She wanted to advance in her career and maybe someday become an executive director. She also wanted to teach at the college level and, one day, write a book. All of which she eventually did!

Your goals will be different than ours, while some may overlap.

For Linda, she knew accreditation was important, so she was determined to sit for her CFRE exam as soon as she was eligible. When the local exam (again, back in the dark ages, when you were required to go to a location and sit in a room with a bunch of people taking the same exam) was canceled, she had to drive to Rhode Island. Her late husband drove while she read books on planned giving for hours during the drive. But the CFRE credential was vital to her, so she did it. The ink wasn't dry on that certificate when she began preparing for the ACFRE process. She had to fly to Toronto to take the test and then to Dallas for the oral exam (which she admittedly failed the first time) and then to Washington, DC during a snowstorm to re-do her oral exam, which she passed this time. Yippee! Again, this was important to her, and certification really helped her tremendously to advance in her career.

During the first international conference she attended, Linda went to a session led by Kay Sprinkle Grace, and, as Linda listened, she thought to herself, "I want to do that—be a speaker at an international conference." She says she was always a frustrated actress. So, she went back home and started to think about the knowledge she had to share with others in the field. She put together a couple of presentations using overheads (does anyone still remember those transparencies and overhead projectors?). After speaking to regional AFP chapters and other professional groups, she was accepted to speak at her first AFP International conference and since then has spoken at many AFP ICONs, as well as in Cairo, Bermuda, Mexico, Canada, and almost all the fifty states here in the United States.

Linda's and Joanne's last two goals are interrelated: They always wanted to share their knowledge, leaving a legacy. For Linda, it was for future fundraisers. For Joanne, it was for future nonprofit leaders. Here's where their involvement in CharityChannel and AFP helped bring this about.

Through AFP, Linda was offered a chance to write several Ready Reference Books and publish her first and second fundraising books. When CharityChannel launched its publishing imprints CharityChannel Press and For the GENIUS Press, Linda really got to fulfill her goals by publishing more than a dozen books and learned enough to self-publish three works of fiction. And she expanded her network enough to launch more than a dozen online courses. These courses may help you advance in your career, and now you can get all the courses for one low annual subscription fee.

Joanne, on the other hand, wanted to do something in addition to her day job, something that could give back to the profession as well as further her career. As a successful fundraising professional, Joanne was asked by a local grant funder to share her knowledge with other nonprofit practitioners in her local geographic area. Soon, she was asked to speak by different groups in her community. Then she was asked to do national webinars. When CharityChannel came around, she shared her knowledge as a regular article contributor, which turned into a book deal. After three books, Joanne was approached by her local university to teach there. She is still in touch with some of her students.

Surely your goals will be different than ours. Perhaps one of your goals is to learn enough about a variety of fundraising techniques to be a well-rounded generalist. Or, maybe you want to become an expert in a particular area of fundraising and become a specialist in this area. Maybe your goal is seeing the world and you'd like to work for an international organization. Perhaps you'd like to be a consultant. Maybe you'd like to write a book or teach. Maybe you want to stay at home with your kids or aging parents and your goal is to work from home. Maybe your goal is to become the CEO of your organization. Whatever these goals are, write them down and develop a plan for how you're going to reach them—and include a timeline.

Also, find a mentor to help reach your goals. Some AFP chapters have formal mentoring programs. Check that out if you are an AFP member. If not, find an informal mentor, someone you admire and respect. You'll be surprised how willing people are to take your call and to spend time with you. After all, this is a giving profession.

So, to sum up: learn as much as you can, especially if there is an area you want to specialize in. Take the online courses that will help you perfect your knowledge. Get involved in AFP, perhaps serving on the board. And in CharityChannel, by contributing articles. Set your personal goals. Good luck with your career! We'd love to hear from you personally about your goals.

Wrapping It Up

- Set goals for yourself when you are setting your annual organizational goals and write them down.
- Use strategic planning methods to identify objectives for each of your goals.
- Monitor progress toward your goals regularly.
- Find a mentor.

Chapter Eight

Moving Up, Moving On

At some point in the career of every development professional there comes the time when some tough decisions must be made. Is it time to ask for a higher-level position within the organization? Do you stick it out in a position that has reached its potential, or is it time to shake the dust from your feet and move on?

In a larger organization there will be more room for growth into positions of increasing responsibility and visibility. In smaller organizations there is often not much room for growth unless you can move into a management position.

Moving into Different Development Positions

Often, when you start in an entry level position in a development office, there is room for growth. For example, if you start as a development assistant, learning the database and all aspects of fundraising, you might move into a position of more responsibility and eventually become the chief development officer.

Some ways to prepare for this growth are to learn as much about the development office operations as possible. Learning the donors' interests and preferences can be helpful when you have the opportunity to move into the position of working directly with these donors. Learning valuable skills such as planning and working with volunteers can also prove helpful if you want to move into a new position in development.

Sometimes you move up the ladder by being promoted from within. One of the drawbacks of being promoted from within is that it is often hard for the organization's leadership to envision you in a higher-level position. Some ways to overcome this are to accept leadership roles whenever possible, to act and dress professionally, and to display an air of confidence that comes with knowledge. Attending classes and workshops is helpful. Enrolling in a graduate program may prove to be a valuable move.

If there is a particular specialty in which you are interested, such as special events, planned giving, or grants and foundation relations, learn as much about that specialty to become the office's "expert" in that area. This could lead to a promotion or even to a new position being created within an organization.

Moving into an Executive Position

Once you reach the highest level within the development office, the options to move up are usually limited to becoming an executive director. While this was not likely in years past, the likelihood of a development professional becoming the chief executive officer within a nonprofit is becoming more and more commonplace. In higher education settings for example, more college and university presidents are coming from the development field than from the academic field.

An experienced development officer will often have acquired the skills to lead an organization forward as its chief executive officer. Skills learned in the development field, such as planning, building strong relationships, and being the public face of an organization are easily translated into leadership positions. Because good fundraising skills are valued in an executive director, organizations are more interested in promoting development professionals into leadership roles than ever before.

Moving to Another Organization

Sometimes you move up the ladder by changing employers, like Joanne did. Joanne's career involved moving up, over a period of twenty years, from a grant writer to an executive director. As a grant writer, Joanne learned about both inter- and intraorganizational collaborations. She needed to articulate new health programs for other people to implement as well as create community support for those programs.

When she relocated due to her husband's job change, she found a job where she did much the same things, only on the other side of the table as a facilitator for the allocation of grant funds, where she learned to analyze budgets, financial statements, and 990's.

Moving up from there, she worked as a statewide early childhood program technical assistance provider, where she honed her negotiation skills. After that, she moved up to development director, where her time was split between fundraising and communications.

Then she moved to executive director, where, for a time, there was no fundraising staff besides her. As an executive director of small agency where fundraising was the only source of revenue, Joanne's fundraising skills served her well.

Some signs that it might be time to move on are:

- The executive director no longer values input from the development officer.
- The relationship between the board and the development officer is strained or nonexistent.
- There is lack of commitment on the part of the organization to developing a philanthropic culture.
- Expectations for the development officer are unrealistic.

Sometimes you wake up in the morning and just do not want to go to work! It happens to everyone. If it is just that it has been a bad day or a bad week, these thoughts usually disappear, and you are ready to jump back in. However, if every day is starting to become a drag, then it may be time to move on.

Often it is because personalities have changed, perhaps a new executive director is on board and just does not understand fundraising or value the work of the development office. Perhaps a new chair has assumed leadership of the board and does not share the previous board chair's commitment to fundraising as a part of the organization's culture. Or a personality clash has developed between you and others within the organization. Sometimes these things can be worked out. But an organization that does not value your input and decisions, is constantly overriding your decisions, or embarrasses you in front of staff, board, volunteers, or even donors is a situation that no development officer should tolerate for an extended period of time.

Occasionally, the chief executive officer feels threatened and cuts you off from relating with the board, volunteers, or even donors. Sometimes this can be worked out with intercession, perhaps from a board member or an impartial mediator. But if the CEO does not allow you a maximum amount of autonomy to build strong donor relationships, you may be doomed to failure.

If the organization refuses to budget adequately for development and sets unrealistic expectations of the development office, you will very quickly become exhausted and frustrated trying to meet these unrealistic expectations. Therefore, it is so important to focus on both monetary and nonmonetary goals for the development office, and for management and development staff to develop expectations together and agree on measurement standards for success. Allowing enough time for a new development office to become mature enough to perform at acceptable standards is critical.

So, when it is time to move on, go back to those networks that you've established. Seek guidance from a mentor. Learn or hone the appropriate skills that will help you in a new position. Maintain a positive attitude.

Many development officers find that after a period of time within the field, they have the desire and ability to move into a consulting position, as both of us have. This step should be carefully considered before "hanging out one's shingle."

Consulting is hard work and many development professionals, while they love the work of development and are very good at it, find the aspects of managing a business, marketing themselves, and maintaining a healthy client balance far more demanding than working within an organization.

While consulting offers you the freedom to work with a variety of clients and set your own hours, it may not be the choice for you. If you are considering consulting, you should talk to other consultants about the pros and cons before making this major decision.

You should also evaluate the marketplace to determine if there is a need for the services you want to offer and then develop a business plan. You also need to consider the benefits available within an organization and determine if you are ready to assume the costs of health care, a retirement fund, and other fringe benefits that will not be available to you when starting out on your own.

In conclusion, the options are many, the organizations are myriad, the profession is growing, and the rewards are numerous. So is fundraising as a career still as crazy as it might seem at first glance, or are you ready to jump in (or if you are already in the profession are you ready to, as the poker players, say, "go all in?")

How to Stay with Your Chosen Path or Choose the Path Less Traveled

- Take time to get away from your work occasionally and really get to know yourself and what makes you happy.
- Investigate all the paths open to the fundraising professionals, talk to consultants and leaders in the field about how they made their decisions about which path to follow and what they might do differently if they had to do it over again.

- Remember that the definition of philanthropy is love of humankind, and if you really understand the world of philanthropy, you will see fundraising as a means to an end and not the end itself.

Wrapping It Up

When you reach a fork in road, take it. —Yogi Berra

- There will come a time in your career when you reach that fork in the road. Should you seek a promotion within your organization or move on to a new organization? Or should you move into a different career altogether?
- If you love the organization for which you are working, you may want to stick it out and try to be a change agent right where you are.
- However, if you have lost all faith in the leadership of this organization or no longer feel you have credibility in the organization, it may be time to shake the dust and move on.
- Having a mentor or colleagues you can rely on for support will help you make the right decision.

Chapter Nine

Your Personal Plan for Success

So, are you ready to advance in your career? As Type A goal setters, we provide you with a worksheet to plan your career moves. So, even if you aren't a Type A, humor us and write down your goals. We'd be happy if you want to share them with us, so we can encourage you along the way.

My current position is _____

What I like about my job is _____
_____
_____

What I don't like about my job is _____
_____
_____

I am happiest being a:
❏ Generalist
❏ Specialist in _____

5. What I need to advance is more training in _____
_____
_____

6. I can get this training through _____
_____
_____

7. I need to join the following organizations _____

_____

_____

8. Here are some ways I can volunteer to strengthen my skills and networks

_____

_____

_____

9. I would like to obtain the following certification _____

10. To become certified, I need to _____

_____

_____

11. Here are the deadlines for my goals:

Goals	What I Need to Do	Deadline
Obtain training in		
Get a degree in xxxxxxx		
Become certified		
Join xxxxxx		

Volunteer in xxxx		
Other goals (i.e. become a speaker, start a blog, write a book, etc.)		
Obtain my dream job as xxxxxxx		

Chapter Ten

Bringing It All Together

Advancing in your career will be different for each of you, which is why we provided you with a personal planning format in **Chapter Nine.** As you can tell from our stories, we took different paths; your path will be unique, too.

So, start by evaluating your interests, your skills, your talents; and find an organization about which you feel passionate. This will make your job easier, more fun, and more rewarding. It will get you through the days when you sometimes wonder what you've gotten yourself into!

Determine if you are happier being a specialist or a generalist, whether you like being a big fish in a small pond, a small fish in a big pond, or maybe even a big fish in a big pond!

Get the training you need to succeed in your career. Both of us provide training in the form of webinars, courses, and coaching programs.

Find a mentor! A trusted advisor can help you find the right career path for YOU.

Pay close attention to ethics. More people than you might imagine leave their jobs because of ethical dilemmas and conflict with organizations that don't follow ethical standards.

Get involved in your local community and in professional organizations. Networking is key to success.

Get educated and strive for certification in the field. It will take some time and a lot of effort, but the result will be a matter of personal pride as well as help you earn more money in the field.

And lastly, don't forget to set goals for yourself, in addition to the goals you set for your organization. Remember that failing to plan is planning to fail!

www.ingramcontent.com/pod-product-compliance
Lightning Source LLC
Chambersburg PA
CBHW071521210326
41597CB00018B/2845